THE BOOK THAT GETS BETTER WITH AGE

OBSERVATIONS THROUGH THE LOOKING GLASS OF AGING

TIM LOVE

LID

LONDON MONTERREY
MADRID SHANGHAI
MEXICO CITY BOGOTA
NEW YORK BUENOS AIRES
BARCELONA SAN FRANCISCO

Published by
LID Publishing Inc.
31 West 34th Street, Suite 7004,
New York, NY 10001, US

One Adam Street, London WC2N 6LE

info@lidpublishing.com
www.lidpublishing.com

A member of:
BPR
Business Publishers Roundtable
www.businesspublishersroundtable.com

Printed in the United States
ISBN: 978-0-9969433-4-5

Cover design: Tim Love and John Fischetti
Page design: Caroline Li
Illustration: Terry Demaline

TABLE OF CONTENTS

FOREWORD

By Peter B. Hubbell

It's said that the purpose of a foreword is to offer words that inspire the reader with the prospect of what follows. As I ponder the topic of inspiration – naturally in the context of aging – I can't help but return to my youth, for it was then that I was touched by the most inspirational person of my long life.

I grew up on a dairy farm in New England owned by my hard-working, Calvinistic grandfather. Pop ruled the barnyard with an iron fist, a fist made firm by years and years of working unforgiving land. When Pop asked us to do something, we did as we were told. It wasn't that us kids feared him, it was more that we feared the loss of his admiration. You see, he was our hero, and we thought nothing of spending endless work days picking rock or baling hay for the simple reward of a trip to town for a soda pop. We worshiped what he stood for, and he stood tall.

For as much as he inspired me as a masculine, hard-working hero, I also remember him for his practical Yankee wit. He was a proprietor of common sense usually delivered with the unintended creativity of a Yogi Berra. While I am reminded daily of his words of wisdom, the advice that comes to mind at the moment is one of his observations on life, "by the time you figure everything out, you run out of time." How many times in your life have you mastered something, basking in your comfort zone of accomplishment, only to be thrust into the awaiting jaws of life's next challenge? Seen in this way, life is not about years but about an endless series of requirements that need to be "figured out".

The Book That Gets Better With Age is a story of figuring things out. Because people of age have lived long lives, they have accumulated valuable experience that gives them an advantage that most young people simply don't have yet: wisdom.

Wisdom is the ultimate form of intelligence because it's created by combining knowledge with actual experience. If we're told that playing with fire is dangerous, we've gained some knowledge. Only when we get burned by fire do we gain wisdom. The experience of trial and error teaches us that fire equals pain, and we subsequently handle it with appropriate care. Wisdom helps us "figure out" things like fire.

Wisdom also helps us to assign meaning to the otherwise random events of our lives. Most of our lives have been spent hurtling through our days, preoccupied with the necessities of living by surviving. We've been prisoners of the moment, fixated on getting by and moving on. But as we age, we find ourselves becoming more reflective. Only now are we taking the time to look back in time, to appreciate the legacy of our lifetimes, but also to help us understand the best way to move forward. Reflection is another way that us older people "figure everything out".

When I was young, I dismissed most of Pop's advice because I lacked the experience to appreciate it as wisdom. It took me a few years to realize just how inspirational he was, and with each passing year, the old practitioner of common sense seemed to become even more impressive. Indeed, the smarter I get, the smarter he seems; alas, we're both getting better with age.

The Book That Gets Better With Age is a chronicle of the wisdom gained with age. It is a gift for all ages, but especially those who are young for it offers a privileged glimpse of the future of life. For all of us who ever said "if I knew then what I know now", this is our offering to those who are willing to learn from our lives' lessons. Laugh, smile or even shake your head at what follows in this book, but above all else, be sure to deeply value the richness that is here for the taking. We only come this way but once, so make sure you do it the right way. Those of us who have already been down the long and winding road that looms ahead of you are here to show you the way. All you need to do is to follow us.

PREFACE

I am a boomager. This isn't something that I just discovered when I retired in 2013 after a 42-year career in advertising. It is the identity I accepted on day one of my career, which started in 1972.

Boomers were born in the post-World War II period of prosperity and optimism from the years 1946-1964. We were the largest and most influential audience of consumers for marketers to appeal to in 1972. This generation was included in the famous demographic called "Adults 18-49 years old".

Baby boomers made the 18-49-year-old segment the most promising target for any advertising, for commercial gain or public service influence. The "lifetime value" of creating brand loyalty with boomers held disproportionate potential for sustainable business growth.

I was hired in 1972 by the advertising agency Dancer Fitzgerald Sample on Madison Avenue in New York City, to understand and appeal to my generation for some of the best marketers in the world, among them Procter & Gamble, General Mills, Johnson & Johnson, Toyota and The Advertising Council.

My first assignment was the public service campaign for the Peace Corps. It targeted boomers (also known as the "Woodstock Generation") who were affecting politics, fashion and music, and who were shifting public views on feminine empowerment, discrimination and America's involvement in foreign entanglements.

Forty-three years later in 2015, I find myself still part of the most valuable generation for marketers and public opinion appeals. But we are not in the conventional 18-49-year-old marketing segment any longer.

Today boomers are in the 50+ age group, the second-largest demographic audience behind Millennials (those born in the years 1982-2004). However, boomers have far more disposable income. This is true in the US and other developed markets of the world with aging populations.

For the past 43 years, I have been engaged in studying how people live and how they think. This informs my views on aging and all that the 50+ age stage of life entails. I kept notes on this during my career, gathering insights from my work with different cultures. I interviewed the remarkable elders I've met as well as the younger people engaged in perception building today.

Back in the early 1970s we boomers subscribed to the idea that "anyone over 30 years of age should not be trusted". We grew up believing things get worse as one ages. Death becomes more relevant and minds and bodies start down the slippery slope of degradation. Though it should be noted that world life expectancy back in 1970 was 60 years, while in 2015 it is approaching 75.

This book brings some perspective of my own and some from valuable suggestions I have been given of "things that get better with age". The time seems right as I approach an age much closer to what I had defined as "old" when I was young,

The learning thus far is simple. "Old" isn't what it used to be, for me, my boomer generation or for marketers. In fact, there's a big future in aging. This precisely explains the opportunity being pursued by BoomAgers, an advertising agency dedicated to the aging consumer marketplace. Founded by advertising veteran Peter Hubbell, BoomAgers has been helping some of the world's top marketers better understand aging and adjust their perception of what "old" really is.

Peter's perspective on this opportunity is well articulated in his first book on the subject *The Old Rush*. In his latest work, *Getting Better with Age*, Peter provides inspiring insights based on his agency's first-hand experience from working with aging consumers.

I am most grateful for the many friends and acquaintances who have provided insights about things that get better with age. I especially thank my "oldest" friend, Terry Demaline (our mothers first introduced us when we were both four years old back in Ohio). Terry's stunning illustrations provide a brilliantly deeper accent on the things that get better with age.

My best editor and wife of 40 years, Kate, gave me inspiration and helped me with the inevitable periods of inertia that plague the book writer.

I also want to thank Peter Hubbell, who presciently founded an advertising and marketing communications agency predicated on insights of the 50+ age group. His agency, appropriately called BoomAgers, is the thought leader in helping marketers communicate with the most valuable generation of consumers.

Many thanks also to all those who offered their ideas on what might get better with age: Tom Burrell, Gail Hollander, Christine Mueller, Tulani Foy, Andy Bielanski, Joanne and Jimmy Berg, Tim and Nancy Joyce, Tom Blynn, a guy in a Motor Vehicle Bureau in Connecticut, my mother Ruth Love, who passed away this year at age 100, my brother Ron and sister Carole. Thanks also to John Flora, Brian Bronaugh, Bob Owens, Harrison Love, Mac Love and Allyse Treier-Love, Eliza Love. Jean and Jackie Plumez, Robynn Dotterer, Pat Sloan, John Pepper, Steve and Michele Wilhite, Sam Kim, Richard Sugarman, Carmen Baez, Karen Zahorsky, Professor Jim Eiche of Columbia University, Dr. Linda Scott of Oxford University's Said School of Business , Lynne Boles, Mike Schrock, Tim and Sue Boese, Joanne Miserandino, Deborah Malone publisher of *The Intenationalist*, Chris Traina, Diana Shaheen, AG Lafley, David Tang, Pully Chau, Bob Norsworthy, George Norfleet, Paulette Clark, Sue Nisbet, Laurence Norjean, Marina Maher, Anthony Rose, Charlie Holland, Ray Uzanus, Rumi Ishikawa, Hiroshi Ochiai, Simon Sproule, Debbie Gotlieb, Bojan Tercon, Judy Trabulsi, LID Publishing and Margot Bachman, a true inspiration who passed away on her own terms at age 97 while I was writing this book.

Looking back, it is only now that I understand what the folk rock band The Byrds meant in their 1967 song "My Back Pages:" *

> "Ah, but I was so much older then.
> I'm younger than that now."

Tim Love
Stonington by the Sea

* Original version of "My Back Pages" was written by Bob Dylan in 1964.

Do not go gentle into that good night
Old age should burn and rave at close of day.
Rage, rage against the dying of the light.

Dylan Thomas

CHAPTER 1
Truth Gets Easy

I met Tom Burrell for the first time in his office in Chicago back in 2002. Tom is founder and Chairman Emeritus of Burrell Communications, the leading African-American advertising agency in the world. Tom spent his career dispelling stereotypical perceptions and images of African-Americans and has been duly recognized for his work by being inducted into the Advertising Hall of Fame.

An elegant and thoughtful man, Tom, now in his mid-70s, was one of the first people I asked about "things that get better with age." Tom listened intently with a slight smile. Then, looking directly at me, quietly and confidently said: "Truth gets easy."

When probed further, Tom, a gifted writer, thoughtfully added, "Truth gets easy. There's no reason to hold back any longer."

Several weeks later I got a phone call from Tom. He said "Got another one for you, Tim. Saying I love you." When asked to explain he said, "It was harder to express this when I was younger. Now, I don't want to miss any opportunity to say it."

CHAPTER 2
Memory Improves

This is seemingly counterintuitive. It is something I noticed when talking to my mother, before she passed away at 100 years of age.

Ruth Love, ever an amazingly positive character, had significant memory loss over the last 15 years of her life. She forgot things within seconds, it seemed, often repeating questions several times in one conversation. As her eyesight and hearing faded, she would ask me who I was. She would always express joy and appreciation that I was with her. Then, 15 minutes later in the conversation, she would again say, "Who are you?"

There wasn't any harm in this, when you think about it. As long as she was safe and happy, there were actually some benefits to having a failing memory. She didn't get depressed or dwell on disappointment. As long as she saw her children, she was fine. This brought her obvious joy, even though she did not remember for very long. My brother, who is a hero to me, visited her every day and oversaw her care.

There is one thing she remembered to say. Each time I asked her "How are you doing, Mom?" she would readily respond, "Well, I'm feeling no pain."

What a blessing to be able to say this at 85, at 90 and on to 100 "I am feeling no pain."

As long as she could say this in her cheery way, who cared that her memory was waning? We all know it is physiologically and psychologically natural for the mind to lose some edge with age. After all, the brain can only hold so much information. Eventually our memories overflow with an abundance of ideas that are hard to retrieve. Maybe, in a way, our memory is actually getting better with age.

CHAPTER 3
Paying Someone to Do a Chore For You

There are many things we grudgingly had to do ourselves when we were younger, like shoveling snow, raking leaves, cleaning, mowing the lawn, moving furniture or heavy boxes, cleaning the leaves out of the gutters, painting the walls, changing tires, making the bed or getting up on a ladder to retrieve something off the roof.

When I was younger, I wouldn't think of paying someone to do these tasks for me as I could easily do them myself. It takes a whole lot more energy now. It sure feels good to pay someone to do these things for me. And it is much safer that way.

CHAPTER 4
Frank Sinatra and Cadillac

Mine was the generation of a music revolution; Buffalo Springfield, Cream, The Four Tops, The Beatles, Zombies, Supremes, Temptations and Woodstock. Frank Sinatra was for old geezers who wore white shoes and had big boats and Cadillac cars.

I still don't own a Cadillac. It isn't my cup of tea.

However, I recently needed to rent a car on a business trip to Los Angeles. They were out of the normal models and offered me a restored Cadillac Eldorado, which I accepted.

I must say, it sure seemed mighty fine cruising down the highway with Frank's "That's Life" blaring to the high heavens on the radio!

They speak to me now. Sinatra's rhythmic tonality soothes me in a world that seems to be spinning out of control sometimes. Better yet, listening to Frank while riding in the solid, luxurious expanse of a vintage era Cadillac is quite an experience, like no other. The experience was far better with age than I had ever imagined when I was younger.

Old Blue Eyes and Cadillac cars go together like freshly baked cookies and a glass of milk. Nonetheless, I still wonder about those white shoes.

CHAPTER 5
Broccoli, Spinach and Kale

Where did kale come from, anyway? Growing up I don't remember it ever being served or on a menu.

But I sure do remember broccoli and spinach and lima beans!

Do these tastes grow on us, or do our taste buds evolve?

How is it that they taste better with age and kale is now used in all kinds of foods, from salads to smoothies?

Hold fast to dreams
For if dreams die
Life is a broken-winged bird
That cannot fly.
Hold fast to dreams
For when dreams go
Life is a barren field
Frozen with snow.

Langston Hughes

CHAPTER 6
Belly Laughs

Go ahead, let 'er rip. It feels sooooo good to laugh!

Why ever hold back? There is nothing embarrassing about letting yourself enjoy a good belly laugh. There certainly is no reason to hold back any longer. When it feels that ironic, stupid, silly or just plain funny, revel in it.

It felt pretty darn good when we were kids and it becomes even better as we age and shed responsibilities and concerns. Don't be afraid to be a kid and laugh again.

Besides, all the health experts say it is good for us to laugh. In some parts of Asia there are even laugh therapy groups meeting in public parks to experience the tickle of a good belly laugh in unison.

CHAPTER 7
Appreciating Differences

Appreciating differences in people, places and things gets better with age. This suggestion comes from my friend and former client Sam Kim. Sam is Korean-American and has had an extraordinary career with the Procter & Gamble Company. He worked in the US, Japan, Korea and most recently was the head of P&G Operations in Southeast Asia from his base in Singapore.

Sam astutely noted:

"Through my experience in working in different parts of the world and with very diverse teammates, I have learned that the answer to all questions does not reside always in being right or wrong, but often also in understanding that the answer can be 'different'.

"This is not about being vague or about being in the gray area, it is about understanding that people can come up with different answers to the same questions. Our gauge for right or wrong is developed from our experience and our culture. When you can respect and harness diversity in recognizing and appreciating difference, then you can truly come up with powerful and breakthrough solutions."

The greater interconnectedness we see today between individuals from many cultures means we must look for what is right or wrong through a different lens. Increasingly the starting point is to first understand and appreciate what is different before passing judgment on what is right and what is wrong.

This is a hard line to follow. It can be uncomfortable. It is easier to judge the world from our own belief systems. But appreciating difference helps us learn more and find better ways to understand our own and other people's needs.

CHAPTER 8
The Front Porch

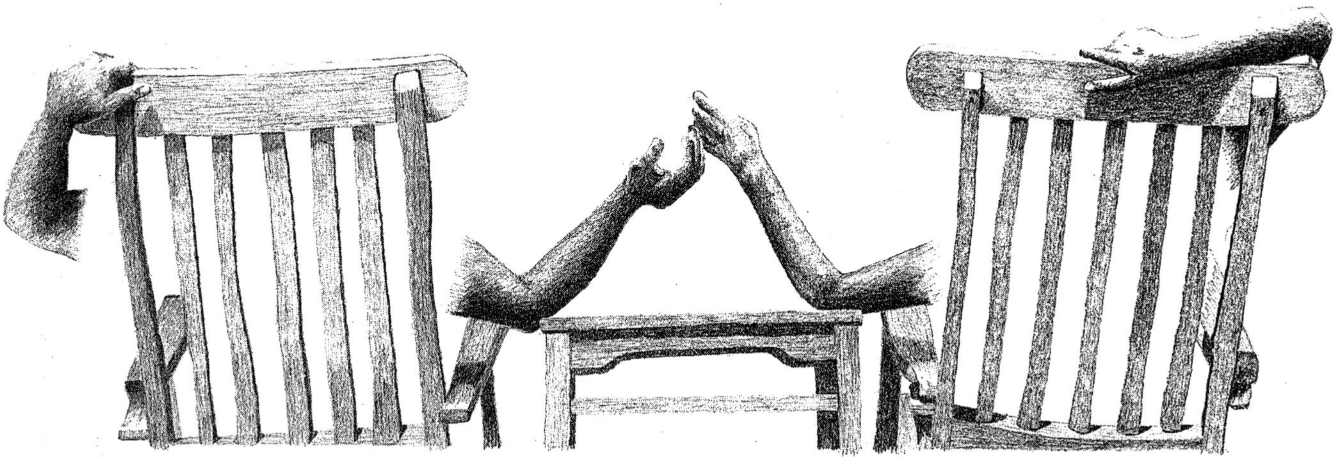

Quiet moments on a front porch with a special someone gets better with age.

This one came in from a former business colleague who has been able to achieve a very successful career in the tough business of advertising, and managed to balance this with an adoring husband and two children.

Her contribution of something that got better with age: "Sitting on the front porch in the evening talking with my husband."

I can still see my grandparents on summer evenings sitting on the wicker swing on their front porch talking and gently waving to friends passing by.

CHAPTER 9
Facing Adversity

This one came in from another old childhood friend John Flora. John is part of the foursome of childhood friends; John, Bob, Terry and I were classmates in grade school and teammates on the various sports kids played in a small town in Ohio.

I guess John is right. Adversity is definitely not something any of us look forward to. Nonetheless, experiences and trials along the road of life do seem to allow us to face disappointments and meet challenges better as we age.

Have you seen my glasses?

CHAPTER 10
Perspective

When I was young and starting out in my first job at an advertising agency in New York, I felt that I could not afford to take risks with my imagination and new ideas. I figured I did not know enough yet to have an intelligent, relevant idea and that it was best to be quiet, observe and learn from my seniors.

Then one day, walking quickly and zig-zagging down the east side of Manhattan on the way to work, it hit me as clear as though all the traffic and noise of the city had stopped, frozen in that moment. I heard my inner voice say, "Hey man, you cannot afford not to have ideas in this business. You can afford to have many ideas and not always be right. But you absolutely cannot afford to be deficient in ideas. Your clients and your company need people with ideas."

As my career developed and my life became more complicated with children, mortgages and college tuition to provide for, I again was faced with the question of how risky I should be with my imagination and ideas. The same thing happened again. I realized that ideas were more valuable than ever and that with the experience I had to support them I should not hold back in unleashing my imagination. It feels so good to express your imagination and this gets better with age.

CHAPTER 11
Being on this Side of the Grass

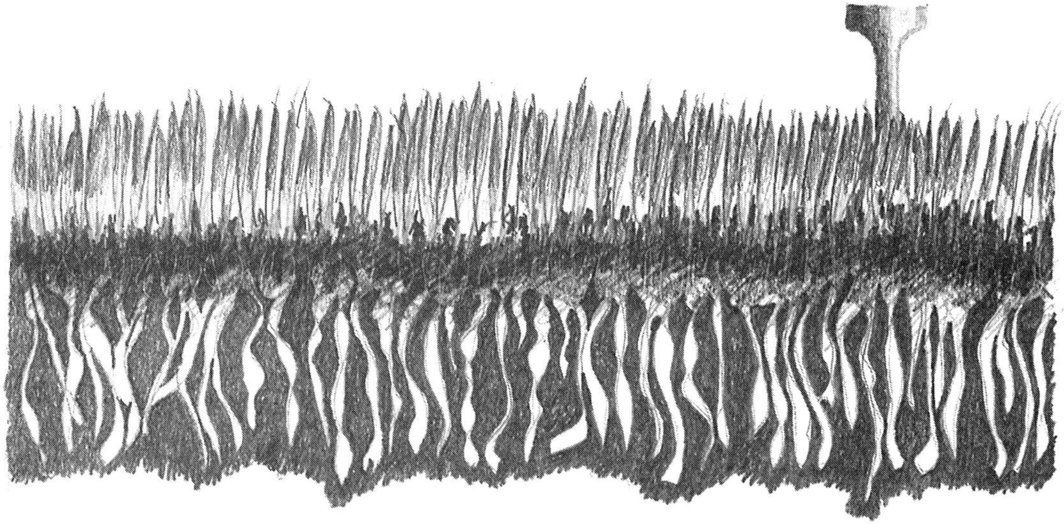

A while ago I found myself having to stand in a long line at the dreaded Motor Vehicle Bureau.

Finally, when it was my turn to approach the counter, I encountered a pleasant clerk. He mentioned something about how long I had been waiting in line. So I spontaneously asked him, "What gets better with age?"

He quickly responded "Being on this side of the grass (not six feet under)" as he quickly stamped my driver's license renewal form and said, "Next!"

He got that right.

CHAPTER 12
The Ability to Amuse Oneself

Illustration by Harrison Love

Contemplation gets better with age.

This submission is from my son, Harrison, first conveyed to me when he was 18 years old. He recently had his 30th birthday.

Harrison said, "When I was young, I was very impatient. It made it hard to spend time for very long without something to amuse myself."

He told me he appreciates having a few moments now, to just sit quietly and relax and think. Amusing himself is getting better with age.

He gets it.

If you sit down at set of sun
And count the acts that you have done,
And, counting, find
One self-denying deed, one word
That eased the heart of him who heard,
One glance most kind
That fell like sunshine where it went
Then you may count that day well spent.

But if, through all the livelong day,
You've cheered no heart, by yea or nay
If, through it all
You've nothing done that you can trace
That brought the sunshine to one face
No act most small
That helped some soul and nothing cost
Then count that day as worse than lost.

George Eliot

CHAPTER 13
Dealing With Authority

My wife, Kate, came up with this one. She says it works both ways. For example, not letting someone's authority, like an officious sales clerk or administrator's, frustrate you, or intimidate you.

Getting comfortable with authority gets better with age.

Our own sense of power and authority gained through experience and the years gives us the confidence to push back when unnecessarily rude or officious people or issues cross us. Seniority has its privileges, in some cultures more than in others, but no one wants to disrespect an older person openly and publicly and often we are the wiser ones in a situation.

We don't just get AARP deals and senior discounts. We should get a certain amount of courtesy and good grace. Friendships, trust and hospitality come more easily, barriers are fewer and more easily breached. Greater and more subtle powers of persuasion also come with age.

We are also wise enough to know the battles worth fighting and those or the people that cannot be changed.

So, why bother?

CHAPTER 14
Highway Rest Areas

More frequent pauses get better with age.

My colleague Peter Hubbell says he is "finally resting at highway rest areas." Here is how he explains this:

"Growing up as a Baby Boomer in the aftermath of World War II, I witnessed the birth of our interstate highway system, sponsored by President Eisenhower as a national defense initiative. What child growing up at that time doesn't remember interminable family trips in the back seat of a hot car? It was also the day and age of Sunday Drives – it's what you did back then. Americans took to the roads in droves.

"Soon, highway rest areas were built to complement the new roads. Most were added during the Johnson administration. Their reason for being was obvious; as more Americans took longer trips, there was a need to provide them with rest and relief so they could continue their travels safely.

"Like most other people hurtling through their youth and middle years, I spent countless hours speeding down the road of life, fixated on getting from Point A to Point B. Metaphorically, most of my life's pursuits were about getting to the next destination.

"When you're racing through life, the highway rest area built for rest and relief serves simply as a relief station. It's somewhere to answer the call of nature, not someplace to actually rest. Why would you even consider pausing when you are living life on fast forward?

"Now that I am both older and wiser, I've come to appreciate what Ralph Waldo Emerson said about life not being a series of destinations, life is a journey. When I plan a trip now, stopping is an essential part of it. I deliberately pause along the way to savor the things that I flew by as I was racing through life.

"I'm heading up to my cabin in Maine next week. It's an eight-hour drive, non-stop, but I'm planning for a ten-hour trip. There are places I want to stop at along the way, and people I want to see. There's even a picturesque rest area in Vermont that I never knew was there. It took me a lifetime to realize that life does get better with age and so, it seems, do highway rest areas."

CHAPTER 15
Forgiveness

Letting go gets better with age.

There are definitely some disappointments in life. Sometimes it is darn hard to forgive, especially when the incident is unforgettable.

Karl Marx said (everything) repeats itself: The first time as tragedy, the second time as farce. I have come to believe that he was right about things repeating.

As I aged I began to realize that a lot of the energy and angst over disappointments, and unfairness encountered are simply not good for me.

Only with forgiveness can we let bad things stop robbing us of our energy and heart. The sooner we can forgive, if not forget, the sooner we can move on.

Forgiveness is one of the most underrated components of life. One of my fellow YMCA Stretch&Go classmates, Ray Uzanus, told me, "the freeing power of forgiveness unshackles the wrongs of the past. It is love's revolution against unfairness. Only you are the loser by harboring an unforgiving mind. Don't carry some-one else's weight; forgive and let them carry their own."

Let it go. Forgive yourself, too.

CHAPTER 16
Loving

Intimacy gets better with age.

Richard Sugarman is a friend who is a licensed clinical social worker/trauma therapist. Richard is a Baby Boomer who was at Woodstock in 1969. He hung out near the pond there where many attendees were sliding down a mud slide and skinny-dipping into the pond. I love talking with Richard and getting his perspective on things.

I asked Richard what he could tell me from his over 40 years of professional experience listening to and helping people, if he could say that making love is something that gets better with age. He became very animated and said, "After over 40 years of consulting with patients of all ages, on a plethora of relationship issues including sex, there is one factor that has a direct impact on the frequency and amount of pleasure people experience with love-making. It is the emotional intimacy between the people. The stronger the emotional intimacy, the more frequent and pleasurable the sex. If there is no emotional connection, there will be much less pleasure in whatever you want to call it, sex or love-making."

He went on to add that there are changes that come with aging that affect the process of making love. Comedian George Burns, who lived to age 100, said "Sex at age 90 is like trying to shoot pool with a rope".

Richard noted there are many products that can help with these issues and some can add an enjoyable dimension to love-making. However, he said these remedies are most helpful when there is a high emotional connection in the relationship between the partners. "If there is a vital emotional connection in the relationship the love-making can actually be better with age. People get better at anticipating their partner's needs, cues

and particular touch points. We know better what is pleasurable for us and our love partner."

"If you're laying in bed next to someone who really doesn't make you feel like the goddess that you are, you need to rediscover what it is that you truly want and need."

Lady Gaga

CHAPTER 17
Pacing Oneself

This may simply be a better way to say, "I cannot do it any more." Pacing yourself gets better with age.

It is not just the physical and mental toll, it is the knowledge that obsessive behavior is not productive. The more you think about it, we are much better today at knowing our limits than when we were younger.

Hope is the thing with feathers—
That perches in the soul—
And sings the tune without the words—
And never stops—at all—

And sweetest—in the Gale—is heard—
And sore must be the storm—
That could abash the little Bird
That kept so many warm—

I've heard it in the chillest land—
And on the strangest Sea—
Yet, never, in Extremity,
It asked a crumb—of Me.

Emily Dickinson

CHAPTER 18
Doo Wop

In an email exchange on the question of what gets better with age, friends Jean Paul Plumez and wife Dr. Jacqueline Plumez sent the following banter:

From Jean: "What gets better with age? Old Doo Wop songs. They bring back memories of cruising on a warm summer night in a convertible with the top down. Perfumed air, soft breezes, girlfriend in the back seat. The Heartbeats doing "A Thousand Miles Away". What could be sweeter?"

Jackie: "Hmmm. Jean was driving and had his girlfriend in the back seat??? Guess I taught the boy a thing or two."

Jean: "To clarify: I am not driving. I'm in the back seat WITH my girlfriend. Who's driving? My good friend

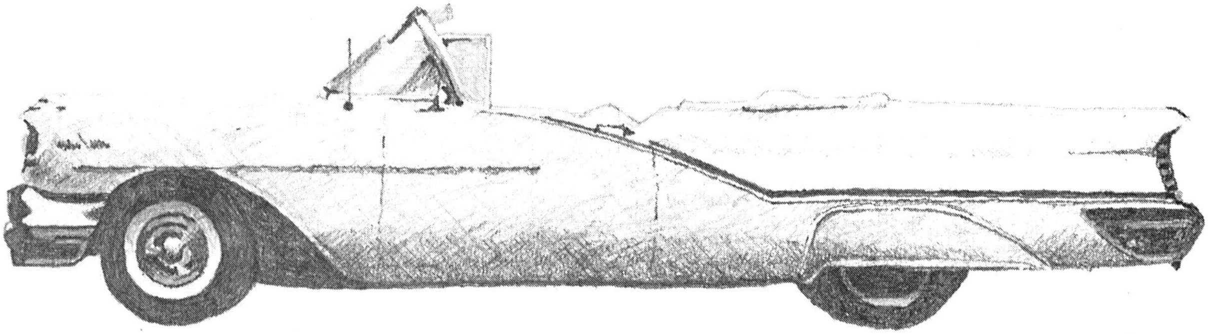

Googie with his 'chick' in the front seat next to him. It's a double date. We're cruising up to New York state where the drinking age is still 18. The car? A 1957 Olds 98 two-tone cream and turquoise. Gotta keep these memories clear."

CHAPTER 19
Feeling Young

Christine Mueller, a business colleague suggested this one: "When you are younger, you try to act older. Later on, when you let yourself feel young and act young, it feels pretty darn good." We just don't seem to do it often enough, do we?

We have always known that youth is a state of mind that gets better and more enjoyable with age. Even when we were younger.

CHAPTER 20
Ugly Shoes

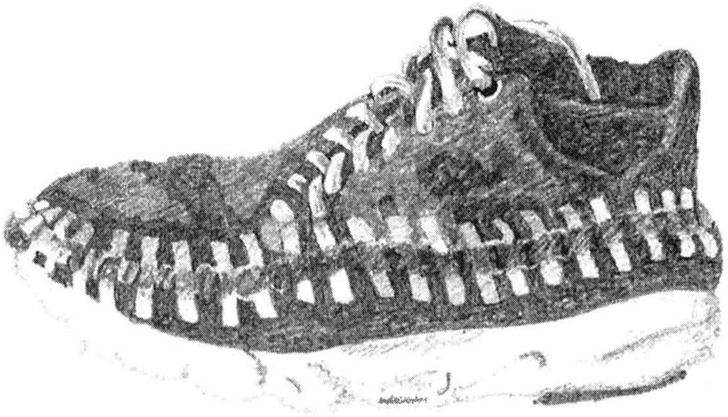

Ugly shoes become less ugly as we age.

In our youth we seemed more concerned with style and appearance than the comfort in things. As we get older one thing that becomes increasingly important is we want our feet to be comfortable.What's really cool is that people always notice how ugly our shoes are. As we get older people want to know what kind of shoes we are wearing. They know, the uglier they are the more comfortable they must be.

CHAPTER 21
Playing Games of Chance More Than Games of Skill

When I was a kid we used to spend Friday nights at my grandparents. My grandmother, Ollie Love, had an enthusiastic love of card games, Bingo and a dice-rolling game called "Bunco". We played for hours.

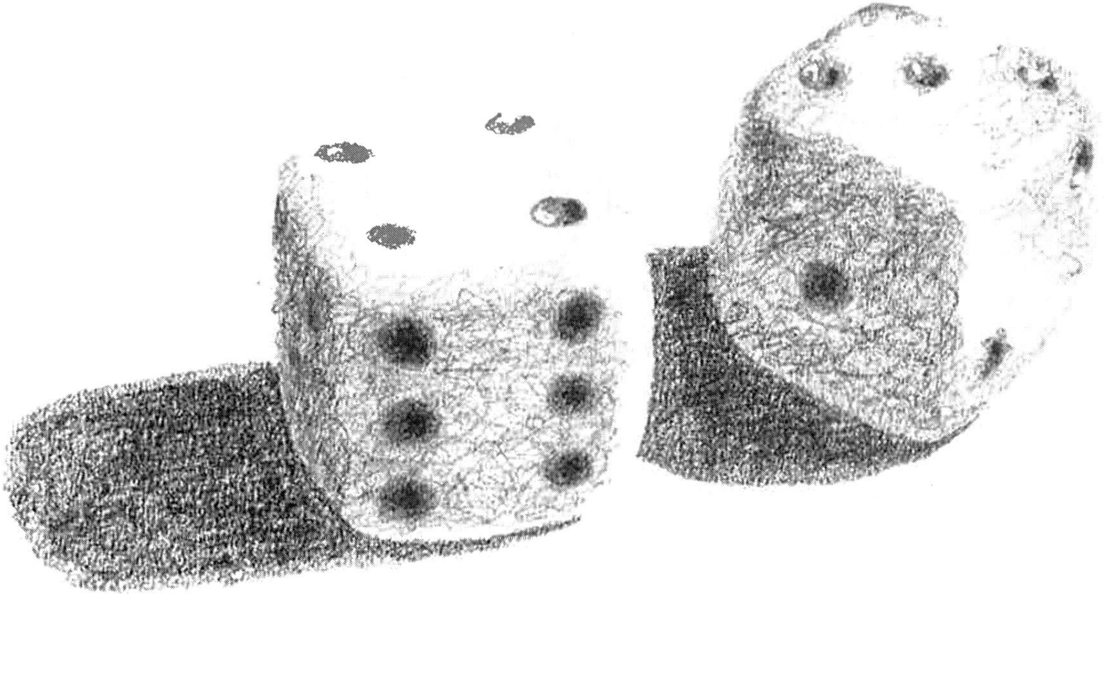

I now find myself enjoying games of chance more than games of skill. I love playing with others of all ages and I am told there is special bliss in playing games of chance with one's grandchildren.

I know one thing for sure, video games are not as much fun. I like the anticipation of uncertainty that comes from games of chance. We don't have to try to control everything. We know that some things are better left to chance.

CHAPTER 22
The Sky

Rising and setting sun, the new day and end of one well spent get better with age.

I look at the sky more closely these days. Cloud patterns are more interesting. I like the varying shades of blues and grays too. It is dynamic and evolving before my eyes.

Now I take a moment to notice the start of the new day with new possibilities and the end of another day, hopefully lived well, reminding me anew, life is as deep and surprising as the sky.

The sky is so much bigger than we are. Paying attention to it enables us to look back at ourselves here on

Earth objectively. I loved paying attention to the Sun going up in the morning and setting in the afternoon in the U.S. But then I moved to Belgium, Japan and Singapore and witnessed the Sun from these distant vantage points, seemingly all the same.

One day it occurred to me that the Sun really isn't going up or down like it appears. It is we here on earth who are revolving while the Sun stands still, shining its light on a spinning earth.

"Think Like The Sun" is a strategy I developed for global marketing. If you Think Like The Sun in life you will see with greater objectivity the interconnectedness and beauty of our Earth community.

CHAPTER 23
Owning You

Knowing yourself gets better with age.

From Ms. Tulani Foy, age 28:
"What gets better with age? Owning you. Finding self, and learning and loving to express you more and better, every day.

"I didn't understand the significance of that feeling until just a few months ago. You see, throughout my twenties, I spent much time and effort trying on different identities — like a costume for Halloween or the perfect outfit for the workday. They would help me fit in.

"I bent. Compromised. Became too malleable, being whatever, to whomever, till I meant nothing to myself.

"And then one day, the stress of it all made the decision for me: The possibility of being something other than who I was to become was no longer an option.

"For some, the transition is more fluid, less chaotic. But the result is the same: You putting your best foot forward with all that is you, and owning it.

"And when you stay honest to that ownership of self—accepting all your mistakes, your successes, your areas of improvement, the strengths that form your foundation, your passions, you live a little bit freer. A little more creatively. A little bit more you, every day."

Really cool, Tulani.

Lives of great men all remind us
We can make our lives sublime,
And, departing, leave behind us
Footprints on the sands of time;

Footprints, that perhaps another,
Sailing o'er life's solemn main,
A forlorn and shipwrecked brother,
Seeing, shall take heart again.

Let us, then, be up and doing,
With a heart for any fate;
Still achieving, still pursuing,
Learn to labor and to wait.

Henry Wadsworth Longfellow
from A Psalm of Life

CHAPTER 24
Cocktail Hour

This suggestion came from a former client of mine early on in the process of writing this book.When asked, why 'cocktail hour'? he replied:

"I am drinking a better class of beverage these days. The wines are finer, the beverages, overall, are sipped and savored. When I was young, we drank some horrendous concoctions, like 'Spodie Odie','Harvey Wallbanger','Malt Duck 30-30' or drinks with similar names that were rotgut and burned a hole in our brains too."

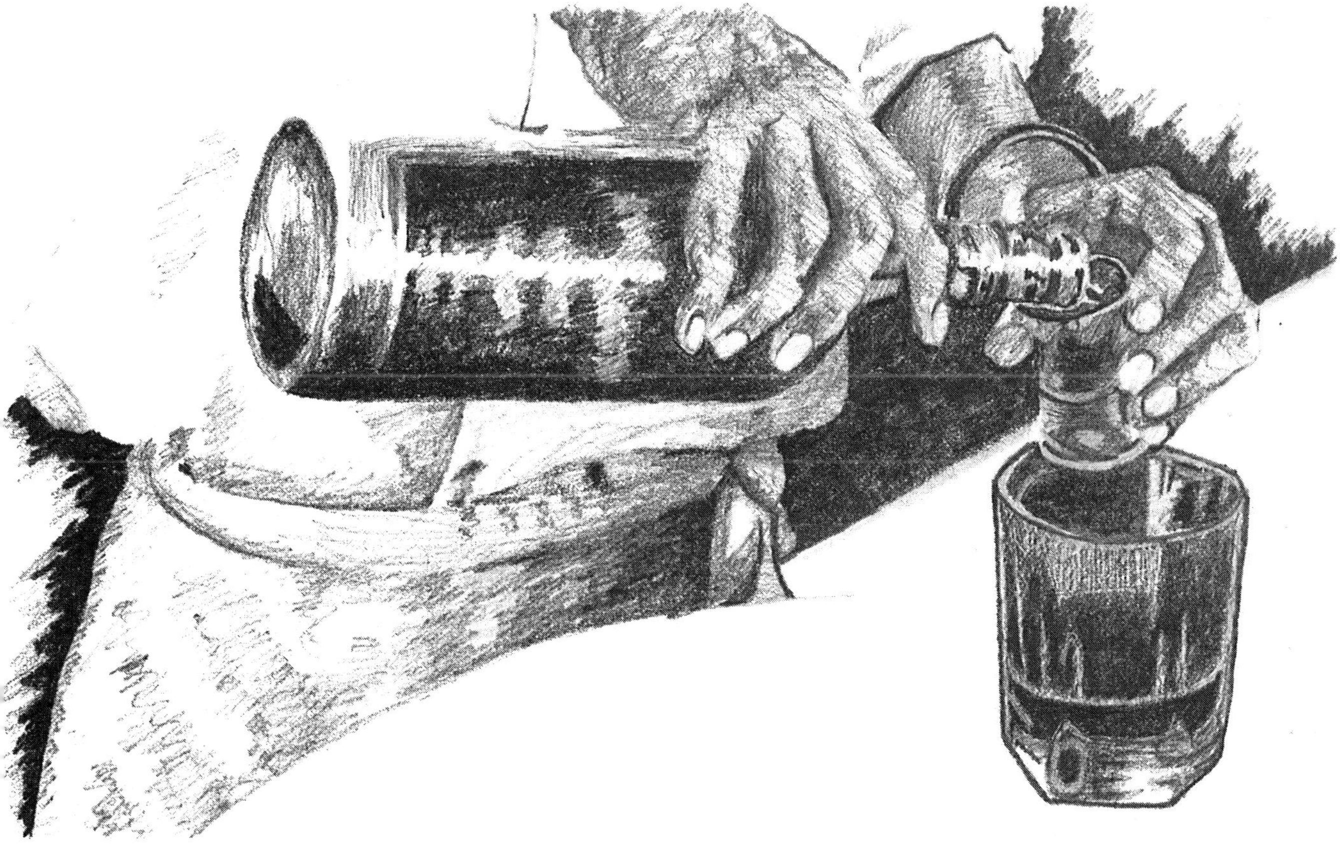

Cocktail hour is now something to be savored. A more appreciative palette gets better with age, in moderation of course. Non-alcohol recipes get better with age, too.

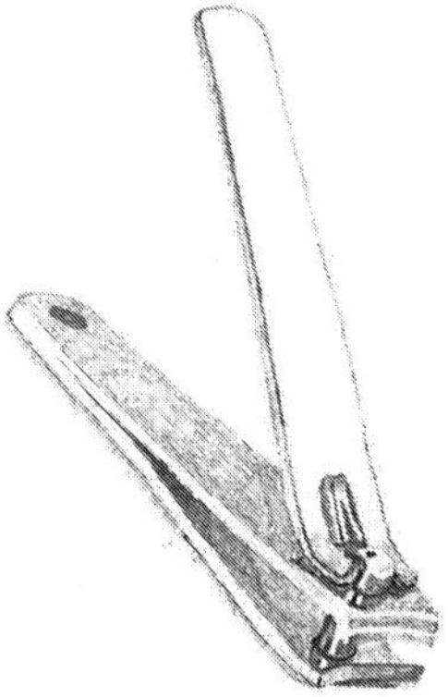

CHAPTER 25
A "Mani-Pedi"

Time for pampering gets better with age.

I really hated having my nails clipped as a child. Later I had little patience for this grooming necessity.

Now, having a manicure and pedicure is sublime relaxation. Warm water, lovely hands with scrubs and oils and often a chair that automatically massages my back.

Besides, I cannot reach down to cut my toenails as easily as I did when I was younger.

A mani-pedi is about perfect now.

CHAPTER 26
Saying No

The ability to know when, where and why to
say no gets better with age.

No is not a negative.
It is a great moment when you
finally realize there is no
shame in saying "no"
to things.
As in, "No, not for me."

No isn't petulant.
No is wisdom.

CHAPTER 27
Doing More *Wants* than *Shoulds*

Being able to make choices gets better with age.

As we age and have other responsibilities, life can seem to grow more complicated. Later on, after the children are grown, unencumbered by as many outside forces, the workplace or familial and social duties, we can focus better than when we were younger. Doing something because you want to, not because you should or have to, has always been most enjoyable.

CHAPTER 28
Driving the Speed Limit

My friend Terry Demaline says he used to be in such a big hurry all the time. The other day, as he was driving his pickup truck across expressways from Tampa to St. Petersburg, he saw several anxious drivers speeding up, weaving across lanes to get ahead of the traffic. "What's the big hurry?", he thought.

Then he concluded: "Driving the speed limit feels just right to me now."

Our ability to be less in a hurry gets better with age.

"Live your life and forget your age."

Norman Vincent Peale

CHAPTER 29
A Nap

Defined by Webster as 1) to sleep briefly during the day or 2) to be off guard.

Peter Hubbell: "Trying to get our seven-year-old to take a nap when the child is tired is a real struggle. Man, I treasure the times when I can take a nap."

Naps are something that definitely get better with age. I look at our cat and am so envious of its ability to take naps. To shut off. Turn the pressure cooker off and go off the grid. I am working on getting better at taking naps.

CHAPTER 30
Doing Nothing

"Chilling" gets better with age.

It seems the older we get the more we have fighting for our attention. The gotta-dos, I gotta do this and I gotta do that compete for our time.

The young get bored very easily and they always need to be doing something, especially in this post-digital world of instant connections, games and instantaneous electronic communications.

I love it when I see an opportunity to just do nothing and relax. It is something I look for now like I once used to look for things to do.

We live in deeds, not years;
In thoughts, not breaths;
In feelings, not in figures on a dial.
We should count time by heart-throbs.
He most lives
Who thinks most, feels the noblest,
acts the best.

Philip James Bailey

CHAPTER 31
Friendship

Treasured friendships get better with age.

My friend Bill Hallamandaris of the Heart of America Foundation expresses this well.

"There is much joy in making new friends, but old friends are like jewels polished by the years.

"These jewels become more valuable and dear to us the older we get."

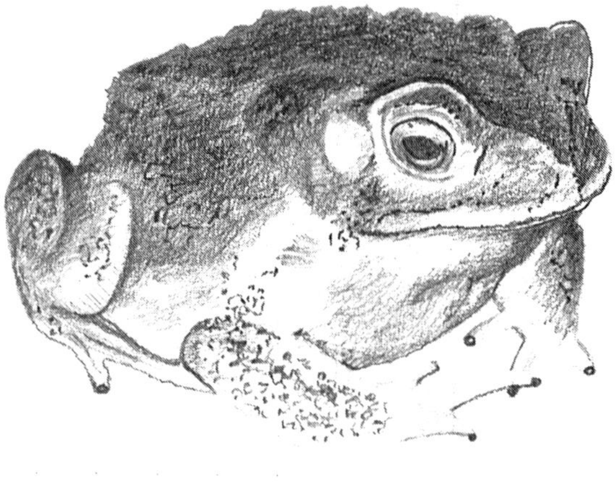

Just like moons and like suns,
With the certainty of tides,
Just like hopes springing high,
Still I'll rise.

Maya Angelou

CHAPTER 32
Siblings

I often argued and competed with my brother and sister in my youth. I was then and still am the youngest. I thought they picked on me.

As I aged, I have been able to look at these relationships in a different context. Our ability to appreciate our siblings gets a whole lot better with age.

THE STORY OF THE ILLUSTRATIONS

When I asked Terry to do the illustrations for this book, I did not give him very much direction. As he sent me each illustration, I became curious about how he arrived at the visuals he did.

What follows are his insights into each of the visuals in the book.

Chapter 1 Truth gets Easy
Tim told me about his conversations with Tom Burrell. I have not met him but I can tell he is not a person who has any problem speaking the truth.

Chapter 2 Memory Improves
Tim's Mom, a fine woman from the south, the woman who introduced Tim and me at four years old and loved her gardening, was partial to magnolias. Thank you, Mrs. Love.

Chapter 3 Paying Someone to Do a Chore for You
Tim hates shoveling snow. So do I. We both did a lot of it growing up in Ohio. That's one big reason why I live in Florida.

Chapter 4 Frank Sinatra and Cadillac
A Tim Love cameo. His family thought he lost his marbles when he came home with a used El D one day and some Sinatra CDs.

Chapter 5 Broccoli, Spinach and Kale
Never liked lima beans. I can draw them, but I can't eat them.

Chapter 6 Belly Laughs
I saw the picture and it gave me the answer.

Chapter 7 Appreciating Difference
This New Yorker cover perfectly presents the issue. Imagine how uncomfortable these differences can feel to each of these ladies.

Chapter 8 The Front Porch
I had to ponder this one for awhile and then it hit me. Kind of the less is more thing.

Chapter 9 Facing Adversity
This chapter hit me as a bit heavy and I felt it needed an uplift.

Chapter 10 Perspective
A silhouette of the remarkable Aunt Margot, when she visited Kate and Tim in Singapore, age 92.

Chapter 11 Being on this Side of the Grass
Nothing special. Just have never heard anything about golf being available in the afterlife.

Chapter 12 The Ability to Amuse Oneself
Asked the author of this suggestion to provide his own illustration. I'm no fool, Harrison graduated RISD and is a fine artist living in San Francisco. Check out his website www.harrisonlove.com.

Chapter 13 Dealing with Authority
This is one that I drew about a year ago, and I felt it fit. You can't argue with that.

Chapter 14 Highway Rest Areas
This is a well-written chapter that I look forward to taking to heart. I had some other thoughts, but felt the sign was all that was needed. That less is more thing again.

Chapter 15 Forgiveness
(Forgive us. We simply did not think this one needed an illustration.)

Chapter 16 Loving
I have not met Richard but hope to one day. Tim suggested an illustration of the author. It works.

Chapter 17 Pacing Oneself
Slow it down. Follow the steady beat of the metronome.

Chapter 18 Doo Wop
What a great time. A vintage Olds 98 convertible with the top down. Doo wop.

Chapter 19 Feeling Young
In St. Petersburg, Florida, we have a softball league for players 80 years and over, called Kids & Kubs. If you're ever in the area, come catch a game. It'll make you smile and feel young again.

Chapter 20 Ugly Shoes
Illustration of Ray Uzanus' ugly shoes. He says they're beyond comfortable. That better be so. They are really ugly.

Chapter 21 Playing Games of Chance More than Games of Skill
Rolled the dice on this one. Wanted to be sure you got it.

Chapter 22 The Sky
Discusses sunrises and sunsets. A sign from England with a great sun was the inspiration.

Chapter 23 Owning You
Beautiful comments. Beautiful lady.

Chapter 24 Cocktail Hour
Just a bartender making a drink. It works, every evening at 5:00pm. Somewhere on the planet.

Chapter 25 A Mani-Pedi
I hated toenail clippers as a kid. Unlike Tim, who is two months older than me, I can still reach down to cut my toenails.

Chapter 26 Saying No
The first drawing I completed for the book. I chose a man with an honest face who looked like he listens well and says "No" easily.

Chapter 27 Doing More Wants than Shoulds
I didn't get this one at all. Sometimes Tim goes right over my head. That's why I love him.

Chapter 28 Driving the Speed Limit
This happens to be my input. Speedometer was obvious. Speedometer from an old love was more obvious. Why 35 MPH? I live on a street that has a 40MPH speed limit. I drive 35 and everybody else drives about 50. Just trying to slow people down.

Chapter 29 A Nap
From Henri Bendel in New York, this eye mask has pockets for ice packs. Cool.

Chapter 30 Doing Nothing
Another cameo. Tim takes this same "selfie" everywhere he travels. Weird.

Chapter 31 Friendship
Everyone loves a toad. This is probably the last toad I will ever draw. I hope.

Chapter 32 Siblings
Based on a photo of my wife's 3 nieces enjoying a day in the Finger Lakes in New York State.

Terry Demaline
St. Petersburg

TIM LOVE

Tim is former Vice-Chairman of Omnicom Group, a leading global advertising and marketing services company. Throughout Tim's 42-year career in advertising his writing and artistic skills enabled him to excel in building relationships with different cultures. He lived in Tokyo, Singapore, Brussels and New York obtaining firsthand experience with consumers for leading advertisers like Procter & Gamble, Nissan and Infiniti automobiles, Kraft, PepsiCo, UBS, Mars and Johnson & Johnson. He also led successful public service campaigns on behalf of Peace Corps, the National Council for Adoption and the Justice Department's crime prevention campaign.

Since retiring from advertising in 2013, Tim has taught at Oxford University's Said School of Business MBA program on "Branding and Communication", he is a frequent university guest lecturer and is on the faculty of the US Marketing Communications College, at the US Department of State's Foreign Service Institute.

He has had numerous articles published on globalization, consumer behavior and cultural understanding. Several of his themes have been published: *Think Like The Sun – The Secret to Global Brand-Building, Our Language Impediment*, and a white paper *Walk the Talk*, on America's image internationally following 9/11.

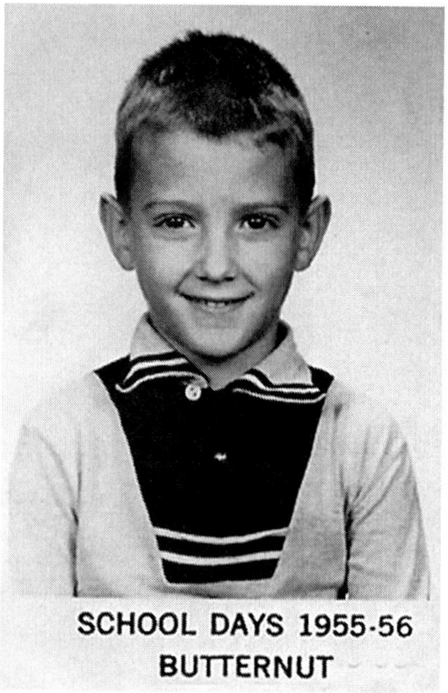

Tim was co-founder in 1973 and first Chairman of the advertising industry's Multicultural Advertising Intern program that continues today. He earned a Master's in Communication from the University of Illinois where he was a James Webb Young Fellow and a Bachelor of Science in Business with a minor in Fine Arts from Miami University in Ohio.

Also see www.timlovesworld.com

TERRY DEMALINE

Terry Demaline studied mechanical design at State University of New York College at Buffalo. He enjoyed a career in that field in positions in design and project management in the large manufacturing and construction industries. He then relocated to Florida and was hired to work on the major re-design effort at the Kennedy Space Center following the Challenger accident in 1986. When shuttle operations were resumed following the re-design, he took pleasure in his involvement with 26 shuttle launches.

After retiring from years of mechanical design drawing, he is back to his love of drawing all manner of subjects. He resides in Florida with his wife.

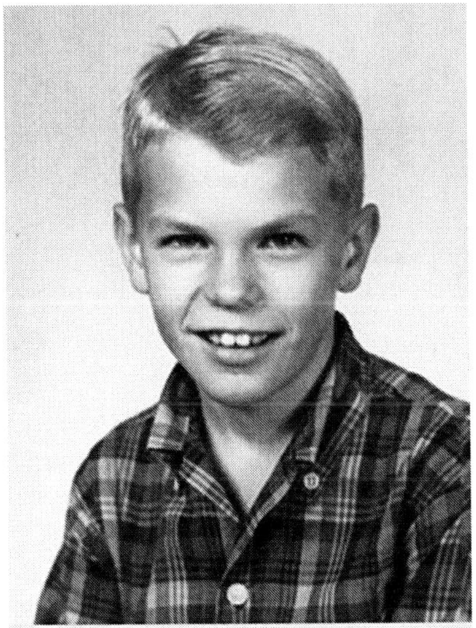

SCHOOL DAYS 1955-56
BUTTERNUT

AFTERWORD

LOOK FOR
BOOK II GETS BETTER WITH AGE

BOOK II COMING AS SOON AS
WE GET MORE IDEAS
AND INSPIRATION.

SEND US YOUR SUGGESTIONS
AND JOIN THE DIALOGUE ABOUT
GETTING BETTER WITH AGE.
@
www.thebookthatgetsbetterwithage.com